TRIUMPH HOUSE
Poetry with a Purpose

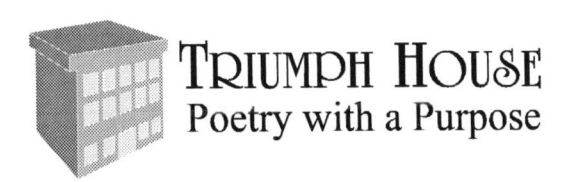

THE KEY TO LIFE

Edited by

CHRIS WALTON

First published in Great Britain in 1997 by
TRIUMPH HOUSE
1-2 Wainman Road, Woodston,
Peterborough, PE2 7BU
Telephone (01733) 230749

All Rights Reserved

Copyright Contributors 1997

HB ISBN 1 86161 139 0
SB ISBN 1 86161 134 X

FOREWORD

The Key To Life is a collection of some of the most inspirational and uplifting Christian poetry that is being written today.

The poets included in this special anthology use their creativity to offer their stories, memories and messages, as they write about the many important elements that make and mould our lives.

The writers are from many varied walks of life, but have joined hands to bring their views together. By doing so they offer a wealth of information and an insight into the Christian faith.

Chris Walton
Editor

CONTENTS

Not Slipping But Sliding	R W Anderson	1
David's Mother	Ivy Russell	2
Second Coming - Coe Fen	Hilary Jolly	3
A Heartfelt Plea For England	Freda M Dixon	4
Thoughts In An Old Church	Joan Franks	5
This Loving Presence	Marion P Webb	6
The New Birth	Virginia Price Evans	7
Together	Patricia Addison Smith	8
Omelette Crunch Day	Kim Montia	9
Path Of Tears	William Roberts	10
Rainbows	Dot Holloway	11
The Big Man	Graham Claimite	12
Send Us Out	J M Rowan	13
The Approach Of Spring	Ella Smith	14
The Magic Of Prayer	Elizabeth Bigg	15
Our Housekeeper	Mariegold Heron	16
In Appreciation	Peter Meller	17
Redundant	Tracey Chantler	18
Shining	David Daymond	19
God's Gifts	V S Humphrey	20
Trust In Jesus	Ty Allbright	21
Reign	Robert W Shawcroft	22
The Ultimate Gift Of Love	Irene Gilbert	23
Our Friend	Margaret Bate	24
The Tears Of Love	Linda Wilson	25
My Lord's Smile	Valerie Copley	26
The Peaceful World	Brian McKay	27
Heaven's Ears	Vanessa L Rolle	28
Awakening	B E Gorman	29
A Prayer	Rex Dawson	30
Painful Lessons	Sharon Eastmond	31
Still With God	Doreen Lough	32
On Our Crucifix	Molly and John Murphy	33
And When . . .	Dorinda MacDowell	34
Heaven's Highway	Ernest Leon Hannam	35
A Neighbourhood Watch	Donald J Price	36

Prayer Is Answered	Jill McLeish	37
Into His Presence	Margaret Jude	38
Don't Be Afraid	Dorothy Ann Parker	40
God's Garden	R Balaam	41
The Thorn	Janet Cullup	42
Beyond Compare	Dawn Register	43
Yes, I Can Remember	Wilma J Gravenor	44
Christ In Your Life	A V Oldham	45
Footsteps	Sandy Broughall	46
Life Without Jesus	S Williams	47
Faith Springs Eternal	Anne Haldane	48
Lost And Found	Priscilla Russell	49
The Cross	Michael Presley-Roy	50
Christ's Lamb	H Anna Hellicar	51
Hold My Hand!	Yvonne Dickinson	53
Faith	Anne Mackle	54
The Christ Of St John Of The Cross	Daphne Foreman	55
Bethany	Ivan Neill	56
Loved In Silence	Deborah Grimwade	57
No-one Knows But Jesus I Know You	Wendy Forbes	58
A Prayer To God	Ann-Marie Wall	59
Mary, Mother Of Jesus	Sarah Harris	60
In Memoriam	Gordon Banks	61
Most Beautiful Things	E M Wollen	62
New Life	Audrey Myers	63
Maundy Thursday	Francesca Greene	64
Fragile Earth	J G Ryder	66
The Gift Of Tears	Patricia Butterworth	67
The Secret Pool	Terri Fisher	68
The Wren	Wendy Skinner	69
Conquer The Darkness	E A Marshall	70
In Little Things	June Atkinson	71
Only One	Andréa Selina Thomas	72
Deep Waters	Sidney A Gadd	73
Quiet Day At Burford Priory	Cathie Hicks	74
Untitled	Rosemary Jacobs	75

My Lost Friends	Jean Hendrie	76
Forever In My Mind	Helen Goddard	77
The Unknown	Mandy Jayne Moon	78
All Praise To God	Janet Cavill	79
The First Christmas	William Edward M Phillips	80
Ne Plus Ultra	Katy Connell	81
My Evening Primrose Flower!	Mary Comley	82
Children In Need	Mena Faulkner	83
Gifts	Joyce Foale	84
Why?	M J Cudmore	85
He's Coming Back	Dawn P Allison	86
The Resurrection	K Maureen Inglis-Taylor	87
Untitled	Joyce Screeton	88
Fiery Shepherd King	Eleanor Ross	89
Just The Hem Of His Garment	Dorothy Eadie	90

Editor's Choice

NOT SLIPPING BUT SLIDING

At the cross-roads of his choosing,
long too late, the urgent stride.
Leaning on the side of caution,
searching for a facile guide.

He talked of suicide, which irked me,
this boy of man and many years.
Now gone the smile, the light, the sweet dream,
lost soul grieving in his fears.

How the wrinkles framed the hoar hair,
drinking from a pliant cup.
Immortal stands time, not idle,
fulfilled being yielded up!

R W Anderson

DAVID'S MOTHER

The passing years had on the whole been kind,
her hair was glossy and her face unlined;
yet there were times when visitors would stare
to see her slumped asleep across her chair,
and gently dribbling in her relaxation.
Nor could she hold a lengthy conversation
since it was hard for her to concentrate
on tales that took some minutes to relate.
Then she would turn her head and look around
for David, who would rise without a sound
and come towards her, ease her in her chair,
see she was comfortable and stroke her hair;
remind her softly, 'You remember, dear,
the folk next door . . . their boy was ten last year,
and everybody told his mum and dad
the party was the best they'd ever had.'
Then she sat up, a sparkle in her eyes,
'Oh, yes, it ended with that nice surprise . . .
something they'd sat up half the night to bake . . . '
Then David told the story of the cake,
his grey eyes tender as he saw her smile
and knew her mind was lucid for a while.
      This was the mother who had been his guide
when he was just an infant by her side,
and everything he was, or hoped to be,
was founded on her love and sympathy.
Now, love was all she needed to repay
His debt of gratitude for yesterday.

Ivy Russell

SECOND COMING - COE FEN

I listened for a trumpet call - and found
Geese bickering on the fen,
Cows lowing and a blackbird's evening hymn.

Upon what angry evening will it sound,
Loud, clear and unmistakable,
Like molten silver falling in the air?

All tired creation groans to hear the noise,
And every song of praise becomes a sigh.
The blackbird calls, 'How long? Good Lord, how long?'
And strident lamentations fill the sky.

Hush, blackbird, He will stand again on earth
And in His coming, all things will be new.
Never have been such buttercups, such stars,
Such fiery dandelions, such shining dew.

And you shall sing to greet him, little one,
And sound your silver trumpet as he goes.
'How long?' you cry. No bird,
No man, nor yet the Son,
Nor anyone except the Father knows.

Hilary Jolly

Highly Commended

A HEARTFELT PLEA FOR ENGLAND

In our beloved country, such a gentle land
With rolling downs and meadows, and coasts of golden sand
Leafy lanes and wooded slopes, where wild life doth abide
With placid streams, flowing through green fields, where timid creatures hide.

Fruit growing in the hedgerows, mushrooms in the fields
Whilst harvest every autumn, comes from garden yields
Most necessities in life, throughout each coming year
Are ours, if we are willing to work, for all that we hold dear.

The chance to get out from the towns, where concrete reigns supreme
With all their rush and bustle, to the country, so serene
Midst trees and flowers, fields of corn, whatever may be in season
So, please all country planners, hark to the voice of reason.

Please leave alone our belts of green, they give pleasure to so many
Such as those who travel to work, to earn an honest penny
Let them have some countryside in which to spend their leisure
To enjoy the natural bounteousness, England's greatest treasure.

There is plenty of space in England, for country and for town
It only needs some wisdom, from those of high renown
Whose privilege it is to be, of service to the nation
We pray that they will be shown the way, to work out our salvation.

Meanwhile we can do our bit, with whatever soil we own
Be it just a window box, or a lawn kept freshly mown
Let's pull up a weed and plant a bulb, just let's do our best
For surely here in England, we are really *truly blest.*

Freda M Dixon

THOUGHTS IN AN OLD CHURCH

Who knows how many prayers have risen
Within these hallowed walls?
A sense of wonder unexpressed
Sometimes upon me falls;
And as I think of all the prayer
Throughout the many years,
Of earnest pleading, heartfelt praise,
Of joys and thanks and fears,
I feel there is a flowing stream
Which carries us along
And turns our worries into hope,
Our sorrows into song.
So as I turn my thoughts to God
And open up my heart,
I'm dipped into that stream of prayer
And then, renewed, depart.

Joan Franks

THE LOVING PRESENCE

I see Him in the daffodil
And in the cabbage too
I see Him in the budding trees
And in the morning dew.
He's hidden in the sparrow's wing
As she takes off in flight
And there among the sunbeams
And in the stars at night.

I see Him in the donkey
Contented in the field
And overhead as storm clouds
Come chasing over Weald.
I feel Him in the tossing foam
Or sparkling golden strand
And in the welcome gesture
Of a friendly outstretched hand.

And when a baby smiles at me
Therein I see His grace
But also mid the wrinkles
Of an old belovéd face.

Marion P Webb

THE NEW BIRTH

Dry ground, sin-bound,
    Parched by the droughts of fear;
Cracked earth, little worth,
    Crying for love to come near;
Lives that are thirsting for cool streams of water,
Praying for God to make Himself clear.

Rain squalls, love falls,
    Drenching the thirsty ground;
Filling, spilling,
    On to the world around;
Making anew the lives that were shattered,
Breaking the chains with which they were bound.

Streams flow, fruits grow,
    Out of the watered earth;
Love springs, peace sings,
    Hailing the end of the dearth,
God making streams to flow in the desert,
Praise springing forth in the joy of new birth.

Virginia Price Evans

TOGETHER

Once you were young, and tall and strong,
Your pace was quick, your strides were long
You went ahead, then paused for me
And then together we would be.

No longer young, and getting frail
Behind no longer now I trail,
My pace is brisk and sometimes too
I stop, and pause, and wait for you.

Soon we may come to Heaven's gates -
One who lingers, one who waits
Then, my beloved, pray for me
That we may there together be.

Patricia Addison Smith

Highly Commended

OMELETTE CRUNCH DAY

Omelette crunch day loomed
And once again my spirits sank
An annual event from which
My culinary skills shrank
Stacks of pancakes tried
To muscle in each time I slept
Whilst lurking in the background
Sugar crystalled, lemons wept
Frying pans aligned each path
Their sizzling laughter spat
And in its jug a smooth
Intimidating batter sat
My kitchen tried preventing me
From entering therein
As batter was developing
A thick and lumpy skin
My children wailed in unison
The batter to lament
And with all they could muster,
Urged me give this up for Lent.

Kim Montia

PATH OF TEARS

I have walked all roads and avenues
Overcome all obstacles and fears,
For many years I had lived the blues
As I trudged along on a path of tears;
I felt so alone and isolated
As my cries for help seemed so remote,
My destiny appeared forever fated
On this path of tears did my life devote.
Overcome with sadness and painful sorrow
Enduring feelings of remorse and grief,
How this path was chosen for me to follow
This path of tears with no relief.

I have persevered and suffered long
But my faith in God has kept me strong,
And the power of grace has pulled me through
On this path of tears I no longer ensue;
Now I live in the spirit of love and peace
And my righteous ways will never cease,
So now I come to the end of my story
As I have shed all my tears on this path to glory,
Take heed good people who have suffered long
Never lose hope be patient and strong;
Let us keep up the fight and wait for the call
For He gave up His Son for the sake of us all.

William Roberts

RAINBOWS

Rainbows come and rainbows go
Where they go to no one knows
Only God knows whence they came
For His promise is the same
I won't destroy by flood again.

The coloured arc that bows the sky
When rain and sun together try
To show us what a glorious prism
Of handiwork that God has given
In the Heavens where He is risen.

Glorious bow of His creating
Wonder of His love in making
Seven hues, each one unique
As nature makes each colour speak.
We praise you God for rainbows peace.

Rainbows go and rainbows come
Each created one by one
And yet man still will wonder why
If God exists He will not try
To right the world *we* crucify.

Glorious bow of wondrous love
God's promise given from above
This gift of peace to every nation
Give praise for wonder of creation
We gaze in humble admiration.

Dot Holloway

THE BIG MAN

The Big Man is always there, but He is never seen
I wonder what He looks like, old and wise and serene
Has anyone ever seen Him and talked to Him face to face
The few times that I've spoken to Him, was only during grace

I suppose that He must listen when we're of troubled mind
Unlike the earthly human beings, He's probably very kind
But how can we be sure He's there, because we cannot see
It's all because of the teachings, of Jesus of Galilee

Through His twelve men, the Disciples, the word of God began
It's stretched the world from end to end, to girl, boy, woman and man
Two thousand years of time has passed and He is still going strong
He'll listen to all and sundry, whether they are right or wrong

And at this special time of year, we know as Christmas time
We thank you Lord up in the heavens, for Jesus, a Son of Thine
And we too want to be Thy children, that one day we might be
Fishers of men, like Jesus, and sit each side of Thee.

Graham Claimite

SEND US OUT

Send us out to be Your servants
As we meet our neighbour's need
Help us Lord, to see Your footprints
And to follow where they lead
May we, by our lives of service
And the words of truth we say
Show the world Your power and presence
Working in us day by day

Set us free Lord, from the prison
We create by selfishness
By our reaching out to others
Use our hands to help and bless
Send us out Lord, but remind us
That we do not go alone
We can only live as Christians
In Your strength, not in our own.

J M Rowan

THE APPROACH OF SPRING

The chestnut tree its leaves unfold
The spring is drawing nigh,
The daffodils are tinged with gold,
The seagulls mount the sky.

The city spires in distant view
We see by morning light,
Their darkening shades approach the sky
As nearer draws the night.

So near the busy city bright
And yet in sheltered vale
We greet the dawning of the spring,
Though still its light is pale.

Though snow clouds still at times appear
And snowflakes dim our sight
Yet glad-some songs of birds we hear
To usher in the light.

We think of Him who seasons planned,
Creator, God, and Lord,
Who formed the hills and valleys
And placed them with His word.

To Him all praise and worship
Let us His creatures give,
May we reflect His beauty
And to His glory live.

Ella Smith

Highly Commended

THE MAGIC OF PRAYER

When the trials of life make you weary
And your troubles seem too much to bear.
You'll find wonderful solace and comfort
In the silent communion of prayer.

When you've searched for the sun with no avail
And long shadows begin to fall.
Remember that God will not let you fall
He's extended His help to us all.

From the magic of prayer there comes power.
It will minimise all your cares.
You'll gather fresh hope, be able to cope
With the troubles that brought despair.
So lift your eyes to the heavens
There's a kind loving Father there.
He offers release, comfort and peace
In the silent communion of prayer.

Elizabeth Bigg

OUR HOUSEKEEPER

She was a plain woman,
Made big by thyroid,
But crowned with curly hair.

She loved our needy son,
Hugged him
And thought him perfect.

When I spoiled her evening out,
She sent me flowers;
When I felt able
To do without her,
She gave me
A bright silk scarf with mimosa.

It was her badge of motherhood.

Mariegold Heron

IN APPRECIATION

Thank You for Your compassion for me,
For taking my place on Calvary.
You were battered and torn then nailed to a cross
You bled and died to bear my loss
Your precious blood poured on my sin
Has saved my life and cleansed within.

Hallelujah Jesus! You rose from the dead
And conquered the grave, Satan's ultimate dread
Glory to God. You have the victory
In Heaven and Earth *all* authority
You're King of kings You reign on high
The fountain of life that'll never run dry

Above all I praise You because of the time
When I leave this world and Heaven is mine.
For when this temporal life is past
I'll find eternal peace that lasts
In glory there'll be no tears or pain
Just honour and power in Heaven's domain.

So until then I'll do my best
To show the lost how I've been blessed,
To serve them like You and love them as well
That they may be saved from going to hell.
I pray they will find the Son You have sent
And realise their need of You and repent.

I know You will help us You said that You would
You gave us Your word, Your name and Your blood
You said You won't fail or leave us alone
But strengthen and guide us until we come home
So thank You Lord Jesus for all that You do
As You died for me, let me live for You.

Peter Meller

REDUNDANT

From my windowsill across the London night
Scattered rows of chimneys stand upright
The cold air chills my heart
The fires no longer spark
Redundant, redundant
No longer of use
Redundant, redundant
Yesterday's source

From my windowsill across the London night
The hum of traffic stirs restlessly tonight
Out and about we are on the move
The hearth of home left behind cold
Abandoned, abandoned
Fend for yourself
Abandoned, abandoned
Keep in touch by mobile

From my windowsill across the London night
I look to the sky where stars shine bright
Man cannot outlive the eternal source
Hide though we may our life is in the source
Alienated, alienated
Created but lost
Alienated, alienated
Loved but aloof

From my windowsill across the London night
The quiet voice of one I know alights
A flame within my heart
A call to radiate
Chosen, chosen
For a purpose divine
Chosen, chosen
To bring warmth to the night

Tracey Chantler

SHINING

How does an angel shine?
Surely it is with shimmering light,
reflected iridescent on the gleaming wing,
beaming in flight from sun, moon or stars,
bent, for light has no mass, not by sticky gravity,
but endless, weightless curvature of space.

What is the light of Christ?
His eyes emit a tongue of flame,
His feet shine, like furnaced molten brass,
His face is as strong, everlasting sunlight,
mirrored on a crystalline, glassy sea,
yet, mighty, all-knowing and very fine,
continually and unconditionally sacrificed for us,
He is also gentle, reflective, softly glowing,
endlessly patient and considerate,
humanely forgiving, full of renewing grace.

Why can we not see the glory of God?
It's hard to put into words, but here's a feeble try.
Surely, it must be nothing
but an infinite, splendidly transcendent and luminous, incandescent,
effortlessly flowing, endless spiritual emission, shining, clear and plain
as the greatest white plate of pure light,
casting airy brightness over all,
yet of such dense intensity that it continuously
consumes itself, seems blank,
to mortal man non-existent.
For, in hylotheistic style,
did it not come all the way
from the Big Bang, in the end
shining on and in us, saints or sinners, originally bright?

David Daymond

GOD'S GIFTS

I am amazed at the beauty I see! My spirit responds
To God's gifts so free - sweet the fragrance
The gift to smell the senses all of which tell the joy to me
I am bereft of any sight, I dwell in the darkness 'til
I am called to paradise, my spirit released, then I shall see
The wonders of God's gifts to me, a light which shows His gift to
Me of sight. So many gifts. The most of all His Son beloved
Who voluntary accepted to be a perfect sacrifice - now He can
Span the bridge to God. He took the heavy load, the pain, the
Sin, and pardon won. He poured His love, His love, so perfect out
Upon a tree and suffered such great agony - He knew His
Father could not stay to look on sin, which He protrude.
To be for you and me. The perfect sacrifice
An advocate, without a fee. Praying now for
Amnesty for whom no other could pave the way
Back unto God.

V S Humphrey

TRUST IN JESUS

Lost alone in pain and suffering, bear you this torture stake for me
the sculpture of my likeness, while I walk beside Thee
have praise in your heart, and diligence in your prayers
your life is not lost or broken, but gently guided up Heaven's stairs.

Ty Allbright

REIGN

Reign in me, reign in me
Sovereign Lord, reign in me
One in Christ, one in Christ
Sovereign Lord, reign in me

Wash me free from sin, cleanse me
From Your heart never part from within
Arrest my soul within
Keep me living in Thy name

Guide me by Thy hand
Keep me walking on terra firma not on sand
Help me love and care for You
Holy Spirit You are true.

Robert W Shawcroft

THE ULTIMATE GIFT OF LOVE

What do we think when we look at the Cross
Where our precious Saviour died,
Can we really truly imagine
The terror, He felt inside.
He was subjected to humiliation
He was spat on and publicly scorned,
He was whipped and laughed at by soldiers,
Who then a crown on His head they adorned.
The crown was full of long spikes
They made painful holes in His head,
And the blood from them ran down on His body,
His precious blood of red.
Oh my dear, sweet precious Jesus,
You did all that for me,
Securing my freedom and healing,
And forgiveness for all eternity.

Irene Gilbert

OUR FRIEND

God loves us each and everyone
He made us the earth, the sky, and sun
He made us the moon to shine by night
And some stars to give us guiding light
He is in every living thing
And when our prayers to Him we bring
He listens to us as we pray
And gently guides along life's way
He's my real Father this I know
And that is why I love Him so
On Him we really can depend
He is our Saviour and our friend.

Margaret Bate

THE TEARS OF LOVE

There was a cross of wood not gold
There was a crown of thorns, not to adorn
There was great sadness, and no real joy
When the Saviour for the world went to die
He went alone, a sorry sight
He went downtrodden, dark as night
He went with tears in His eyes
Alone, the Saviour for the world went to die
I feel His pain when standing there
He's proved by love, the cross is bare
Come Father now and claim Your Son
To prove that life, o'er death has won.

Linda Wilson

My Lord's Smile

When I approach Heaven
and the gates open wide,
my Lord smiles down on me
and says 'Come inside,'
then I'll know that my efforts
were all worthwhile,
when I see my Lord smile.

When I hear the angels singing sweet
praising their Heavenly King,
and I kneel at last at His holy feet
my own song of praise I will sing,
forgotten will be all life's hardships and trials,
when I see my Lord smile.

No more the anguish and heartbreaking pain
will I feel when that day has come,
I'll be with all my dearest loved ones again
heartache and grief now all gone,
all this when my Lord says 'Come to me child'
and I see His wonderful smile.

Valerie Copley

THE PEACEFUL WORLD

A peaceful world I would like to live in
wake up in the morning and hear the birds singing.
walk down the path and smell the fresh flowers as
they blossom in spring.
To meet people with a big smile saying, 'Good morning
Isn't it a peaceful, bright, lovely day.'

A world where there's no hatred, fear,
Discrimination, war and famine, drugs and diseases.
But where there is peace and harmony, caring and sharing,
Love and comfort, helping and showing the right way in life.
A world where man doesn't destroy nature and wildlife,
But they can live together as one.
A world where people don't say the wrong things to each other -
Offending and upsetting this can be.
A world of no sin and shame but of purity and righteousness
for all mankind to live in.
A world where people don't live by the gun or bomb,
but start living for Jesus.
There can only be peace through knowing the One who gives it.

Brian McKay

Heaven's Ears

Heaven has a special way of listening to prayers
It hears the unspoken words, it attends our fears
It listens when no-one else would care to
It's always listening just for you

It knows your voice
It recognises your sound
It can tell when you are happy, or sad
It knows when you are bound

It hears a whisper
It translates a groan
Heaven hears the burdens you bear
That only comes out as a moan

The vibes of hurt it picks up
Rejection's pain it bears
There's nothing that can happen to you
That can escape Heaven's ears

When your heart is heavy
And you can't find the right words to pray
Heaven's ears come to your heart
And listen to what it has to say

The mind is confused, and doubt sets in
You want to stop, give up and give in
Heaven's ears pick up on this too
And soon, somehow you will get through.

Vanessa L Rolle

AWAKENING

Leaving me to the pleasant early
Morning silence of the room
He gently closed the door behind him.
Squares of shimmering pale sunshine, pearly
Yellow reflections bathed the entire opposite wall.

I felt the warmth of ripening
Spring air through the glass panes,
Coaxing insect-laden blossoms, pink and white
To welcomely reach out singing
Their joy to the new day's birth.

Content in my reflective thoughts and
Enveloped in the warmth and quiet
I was not alone. Butterfly wings beat
Inside me, and I placed a hand
Over another new life to be born.

B E Gorman

A Prayer

Oh! Take him Mother Earth to thy cool breast
Enfold him in thine arms for ever more to rest.
His day is o'er, his little race is run:
No more the evening walks, no more the playing in the sun.
To thy dark chamber, Mother Earth, he comes;
Prepare his dreamless bed in his last home.
Close fast his dear brown eyes for ever more;
His soul is fled beyond the golden door.

Rex Dawson

PAINFUL LESSONS

I heard some news the other week
it really broke my heart,
the thing that really gets me
God knew right from the start.
He knew that it would happen
and that it would cause pain
but it seems without this suffering
there would be no gain.
Although it's not a lovely thought
I'm afraid to say it's true
that if we do not suffer
we don't grow - in truth.
Even though we suffer lots
and the pain seems hard to bear
we do have a Heavenly Father
to talk to and He will share.
He will give to us His peace
and strength and courage too
and hopefully in the course of time
this will get us through.

Sharon Eastmond

STILL WITH GOD

To read His word is to learn His way,
To talk to Him is to pray.
To search Him out is to seek His face,
To find Him is to see His grace.

I can talk to God each and everyday,
Tell Him my problems, thanks to Him pay.
I can ask for help and healing too,
For this I know my God can do.

But sometimes I need just to be still,
To listen to God's voice, seek His will.
To be in His presence at total rest,
I feel so safe and by Him blessed.

To just be in His presence is so good,
I would stay there always if I could.
For God offers us joy and such peace,
As I sit with God all worries cease.

Doreen Lough

ON OUR CRUCIFIX

Aware of wonder we hang
Nailed to the crucifix
With Jesus we hang
Absorbed in mystery
Side speared open
Many wounds unknown
Are shown
In our meditation
God's love we find
Now through Jesus' His Son
With all of us
On the crucifix
We willingly plead
Please dear God
Help us to love
To worship Jesus
Here on His crucifix.

Molly and John Murphy

AND WHEN...

And when the world has done with me
When my eyes rest and close
Dear Lord, protect and shelter me
And guide me towards those

Whose going before may light my path;
Unknown to me 'twill be,
Oh! I will tread it willingly
To seek repose with Thee

Though I shall feel the hurt to part
With those I love on earth,
I pray your mercy 'compass them
That they may know new birth

As once did I! Oh! Glorious time!
I pray those I love true
Would, by Your mercy and Your grace,
So burn with love for You!

Dear Master! Always You have been
My champion and my friend
Lead me now through my darkest night
My earthly life to end

And do not cry, my dearest ones!
I hear the Saviour's voice
He's calling me, thus, heavenward
I cannot but rejoice!

The Lord is kind; He feels your pain
This day; He leadeth me
That I in turn, when it is time
May light the way for thee!

Dorinda MacDowell

HEAVEN'S HIGHWAY

I saw a beautiful garden,
Filled with people I had known,
With arms held out they are saying,
Come in, you are not alone,
In this paradise of beauty,
I will dwell forever more.
For it is God's wish that I enter,
Through Heaven's golden door.

Ernest Leon Hannam

A Neighbourhood Watch

There's a neighbourhood watch round our residence,
    Security is assured
And just where is our hope and our confidence?
    We trust in the living Lord.
Perceiving where all of the troubles may start,
    The sins and the lawlessness,
They begin, so He says, in the human heart,
    The same place He seeks to bless.
Through the Lord God alone, can the conflict cease,
    When we are with Him allied,
We shall start to be channels of His true peace
    And tell of His mercy wide.
All the neighbours will watch, as God's only Son
    Through His spirit comes to earth
And the blessings that flow from what He has done
    Are witnessed for their true worth.

Donald J Price

Prayer Is Answered

Every single prayer that's uttered -
Shouted out or quietly muttered -
Gets the very same attention
Whether filled with joy or tension.

Every prayer does not receive
The response for which we plead.
He's contemplated every plea
To give the best to you and me.

His answer may not be our will,
But His omniscience shows skill
That we mere mortals may not see
Is just the thing to set us free.

Our firm belief in this decision
Depends upon His greater vision.
We know He answers every prayer
And all our problems He will share.

If your request you think is fair
And His response is hard to bear,
If you've prayed in Jesus' name
And Scripture's promise now you claim,
If you've asked on bended knee
From your burden to be free,
Remember God can see the whole
And by His grace you'll reach your goal -
But in His way and timing too
For He has only Love for you.

Jill McLeish

INTO HIS PRESENCE

There is here a stillness:
A tangible stillness
Where everything of the world
Is stilled and stopped.
Not the stillness of emptiness
Or nothingness
As in death viewed
Without hope,
But a stillness alive
With the stupendous wonder
Of infinity touching the finite,
Eterenity captured in time
Releasing time into eternity.

Woven into this stillness lie
Years of trembling prayers,
The hours of praise and blessing,
Freely poured forgiveness
And the flowing tears, -
Each teardrop known and
Counted by God.

Steeped in the stillness,
Sifted through repentance,
The mystery of His perfect healing power.

All this and more is here,
Left like a fragrance
Misted into the air,
Each variegated rainbow-strand
Diffused together
Into the one dazzling light
Of the Son
Who whispers to you:
'Lo,
In the stillness,
I am here!'

Margaret Jude

DON'T BE AFRAID

Don't be afraid
The Lord is here today
Just open up your heart
and throw all hate away

Don't be afraid, listen to what
He says, follow Him right now
in His caring ways.

Oh don't be afraid let Him
Enter in, to lighten up your
darkness and cleanse you from
all sin.

Don't be afraid, He's here all
around, listen for a moment
you will hear His sound
So don't be afraid.

Dorothy Ann Parker

GOD'S GARDEN

The whole world is God's garden,
Where he puts all His creatures to dwell,
Such beauty of line, it holds us in a spell
In awe that suspends Earth and Heaven.

While held in this thrall
Our lives are enriched,
By the knowledge that He is our Lord;
And the gifts of His country is free to us all

Now let's give freely to God
What He has first given to us,
Let us ensure that His voice is heard;
When we sing praise for all His good gifts.

R Balaam

THE THORN

I am the thorn that
Caused blood to flow
When I pierced His sacred brow.

I watched the nails
Hammered into hands
Which blessed the perpetrator.

Saw feet which walked
On the stormy sea
Nailed to a tree.

I sighed as the virgin
That bore Him
Knelt in tears at the foot of the cross.

I flinched when the spear was driven
And His side riven
Marvelled when all were forgiven.

I saw all tremble as the sky
Turned black
And the temple veil rent in twain.

Yes, I made Him bleed
But the blood that was shed
In all innocence,
At Calvary
Was not for me
But you.

Janet Cullup

BEYOND COMPARE

Roaming, diverting, blown like a leaf in the wind,
You, O Lord, are the Rock.

We change in time and circumstance,
You, O Lord remain steadfast.

We strive to be the best, number one,
You, O Lord, are beyond achievement or dream.

Beasts of uncontrollable passion and desire,
You, O Lord, discipline and provide purpose.

Bored and tired, stressed and depressed,
You, O Lord, put each breath in our bodies.

We follow a short-sighted plan, treading on others
You, O Lord, have an eternal plan for all.

We learn by mishap and mistake,
You, O Lord, hold wisdom.

Teenage fans of conformity; nurtured manipulators,
You, O Lord, the creator and lover of individuals.

We constrain life to logic and experience,
You, O Lord, know no boundaries.

We seek comfort in the plain and mundane,
You, O Lord, work extraordinarily.

An insurmountable gulf of difference,
You, O Lord, have bridged the gap.

Dawn Register

YES, I CAN REMEMBER

We too have loved, and laughed and dreamed,
And in our childish hearts have felt the joy that was the birth
of spring.
Each sparkling moment, magic, seemed to sing sweet promises,
To breathe of the beauty our lives would bring -
When we were only young.

Yes, we remember the summer rain,
The dances of rainbow butterflies.
The scent of garden roses, the heady perfume of June . . .
And lived over and over again.

In sweet dreams and fond memories -
Now, we can only talk of our youth.
That which vanished all too soon.
Yes, we smile, we remember, we grow old.

Wilma J Gravenor

CHRIST IN YOUR LIFE

As you travel around.
In this world I know,
There are pleasures of Earth,
In each place we go,
Oh so many trials,
We all have to face.
But with Christ in our lives,
We know we are safe.

So many times,
We try to find
A remedy for peace of mind,
But there's only one answer,
From this world of sin,
And if you're without Christ,
You just cannot win,

Have you Christ in your life,
Is He right in your heart,
Are you with Him, always,
Never to part.
Have you taken your stand,
With the Christian band,
For if you're without Christ,
You're on sinking sand.

A V Oldham

FOOTSTEPS

To take a step forward
We take a step back
For lessons to learn
Know we're on the right track.

The footsteps are harder
With lessons well learnt
Nothing comes easy
They have to be earnt.

One step ahead
One step beyond
It can be so easy
To walk for so long

The footsteps we take
Can easily be shown
The knowledge we gain
Into the unknown.

So follow His footsteps
He showed us the way
The footsteps are there
Each time that we pray.

But make your own footsteps
Each lesson you learn
To pass to another
The footsteps are shown.

Sandy Broughall

LIFE WITHOUT JESUS

What is life without Jesus
A life held in sin and death
What is life without Jesus
A life filled with emptiness;
Nothing left

What is life without Jesus
Confusion, loneliness and strife
What is life without Jesus
To live on your own understanding

What is life without Jesus
To live without the promises God has said
What is life without Jesus
Where your spirit is completely dead.

What is life without Jesus
That you chose to be lead by your sight,
And not to follow Jesus who is
The true light
Living powerless and in darkness,
Not having a relationship with God
Not knowing the experience of His grace
And love.

Conclusion: those who live in Christ
Are blessed,
For we have found the way
Now let's keep steadfast
And not be tempted to stray.
Because Jesus is the only way.

To live a life without Christ
You must pay the price eternal
Damnation for the rest of your life.

S Williams

FAITH SPRINGS ETERNAL

Deeper ever deeper I know I cling to you
Through the trials of living
My life is entwined
And colours everything I do.
Accept the love I offer,
It gives me peace you see,
Oh Jesus, gentle Jesus
Let me follow Thee.

Anne Haldane

LOST AND FOUND

I often wonder why we suffer in this world, it wasn't the Lord's fault but that is why He came.

Many years have come and gone They tell me He died at the age of thirty-three.

I listened to my grandfather as he told parables by the sea.
I was only young a child, every word comes back to me.

When I am low and lost I say a little prayer and it comes from the soul.

Jesus has never let me down even when it is hard to kneel down.

I kneel down praying for forgiveness.

I feel so humble and hypocritical. Please dear Lord I didn't believe.

One day at a time, the saying so true but as a little girl
I ran to You. Not understanding where to go.

I would pray for steadiness He would say.

To see the world through His eyes. Jesus was not afraid of dying.

Dear Lord miracles do happen, with you by my side I am not afraid of dying or crying. I am no longer lost.

I found somebody and yes it is You.

Priscilla Russell

THE CROSS

'The grace of our
*Lord Jesus
Christ*, and the
love of *God*,
and the fellow-
ship of the
Holy Ghost
be with us all,
evermore. Amen.'
'Cross forehead, breast, we make the Christ sign,
thereby his purpose-path of sacrifice, enshrine.
May body, mind and heart by caring love combine,
delete self-centred 'I' through Spirit power benign.
Guide and steer
in thought, word,
deed, when oft
we do veer from
decent need Tho'
many our errors,
Lord intercede.
Never will be our
plaints ignored,
whatever secret
prayer implored.
On everyone His
grace; blessed be
this year of our
Saviour Lord.

Michael Presley-Roy

CHRIST'S LAMB

A wandering lamb, small and grey,
I need a Shepherd near,
To care and hold in powerful arms,
To teach me I am dear.

I call the Shepherd when I'm hurt,
And know that He will hear.
If I listen with my heart
His voice, though soft, is clear.

He lets me pasture for myself
But when I go my way,
His eyes are on me, watching close,
So I don't too far stray.

If I lose the path He wants
I don't know where I am.
The faith He gives me in my heart
Reminds He'll save His lamb.

He always understands, I know,
My strayings every day.
Forgiveness is the balm He gives
When I confess I stray.

After a fall, I look towards
The Shepherd whom I keep
In my heart, He grants my needs:
Strength, grace, and sleep.

I remain my Shepherd's lamb,
A pity I'm so grey,
But with His powerful care I may
Be lighter grey one day.

Far from Him the shade is bleak,
Like dark on moonless night.
When He pours His love on me
The dark grows into light.

Commended

Shepherd, praises for your care
Of all the lambs on Earth,
Help all souls into your fold
And give us Christian birth.

H Anna Hellicar

HOLD MY HAND!

Please child
Hold my hand
Before I die
And leave this land
Before this body of misery
Breathes its last
And sets me free
Hold my hand don't
Ask why
I gave you life before I died
Remember all the good I've done

Hold my hand
I'm leaving son

Whisper with my dying breath
You can share what I have left
Hold my hand
I have to go
Up with the angels
Where chariots swing low
Hold my hand
Please don't cry
My very last breath
Turned into a sigh
I hate to leave you
In this sorrow
But God won't wait until
Tomorrow.

Yvonne Dickinson

FAITH

There is a God up above, I believe that is true
But not everyone thinks that way
Not everyone has the gift of faith
This gift keeps me sane day by day.

I believe in prayer and in its power.
Prayer, a relationship with God.
We both talk, chat and listen
Life's not over, once we're under the sod!

When I look at this Earth and its beauty
I marvel at the sky, land and sea
When I consider mankind, what a creation!
I believe a superior being there must be.

My faith is a gift and I'm thankful.
It's unaffected by clerics who stray.
They're just human and therefore can err.
God's divine, so I believe and I pray.

Anne Mackle

THE CHRIST OF ST JOHN OF THE CROSS
(From the painting by Salvador Dali)

He sees the world, a chasm at His feet;
Yet ever high above the turmoil and the din,
The everlasting arms are stretched wide, shelteringly;
And love looks down in yearning, pitying sin.

He hears the myriad cries of Earth's distress;
A ceaseless clamour, rising cry on cry;
The hungry, lonely, sick and those that mourn:
Yet ever love, they by their sins do crucify.

He sees the fisher-folk and men that sail the seas,
Leaving their well-known coasts to brave the unchecked deep,
And hears their cries when high the storm-wind breaks,
And keeps their feeble craft safe while they sleep.

He sees men fight with men for right or wrong,
And hears the cries of those by war bereaved;
Yet His the hands dragged by the weight of sin not His;
His broken heart that never sin conceived.

He sees the woes and follies all of men,
But too He sees the hands that lift in prayer:
A murmuring louder grows, like thunder rolls,
Assails the heart of Him who listens there.

With broken heart, torn hands and bleeding feet,
Hangs the eternal man on the eternal rood;
The sinless man bearing the sin of all the world,
Hangs between men and the just wrath of God.

He sees the world beneath, a chasm deep and wide;
He sees the kingdoms, nations, captains; rise and fall;
Yet ever hangs, for man's deliverance,
That great compassion over-sheltering all.

Daphne Foreman

BETHANY

There's no more touching picture of devotion
Than that displayed at Simon's festive board
Where Mary broke the box of costly spikenard
And poured it on the head of her dear Lord.

The fragrance filled the room where they were gathered
There Mary's tears flowed o'er the Master's feet
As with her tresses tenderly she bathed them
Did mortals ever such devotion meet.

The guests' response was harsh and so uncaring
What waste is this indignantly they cried
Better than the poor had the advantage
By this being sold and given to their need.

And Simon where is your wonted hospitality
No kiss of welcome for your honoured guest
His feet to bathe no water you provided
Yet you permit your guests to thus protest.

The Lord now reprimands those heartless critics
Swift to condemn but Oh so slow to see
Against the day of my decease and burial
This offering has been prepared for me.

Did Mary have an inward intuition
That head with piercing thorns would soon be crowned
Those feet that once were rocked in Bethlehem's cradle
By cruel nails would to the cross be bound.

Mary has won her place with the immortals
Where'er the Gospel sounds her deed is told
Thus is fulfilled the prophecy of the Master
Her memory now is richer far than gold.

Ivan Neill

LOVED IN SILENCE

Only a breath between us
No need for a word to be spoken
We sit in the stillness together
You with hands and feet scarred by cruel nails
I bathed in your forgiveness
We are one, as your Holy Spirit gives me life
I am your child, you are my father
And I am enveloped in your love.

Deborah Grimwade

NO-ONE KNOWS BUT JESUS I KNOW YOU

No-one knows what I am thinking but Jesus I know You do,
When my words I cannot find, my thoughts are clear to You,

No-one knows what I am thinking but Jesus I know You do,
When I need a helping hand there's no other on this land who can help me like You do.

No-one knows what I am feeling but Jesus I know You do,
When no-one else understands, it's You who I turn to,

No-one knows what I am feeling but Jesus I know You do
When I'm feeling hurt inside, when someone has made me cry, no friend will do but You.

No-one knows how much I love You but Jesus I know You do,
When I'm scared and on my own I remember I have You,

No-one knows how much I love You but Jesus I know You do.
You blessed me with Your sacred light, inside of me it shines so bright,
You are the beauty in each new day,
You are the warmth that soothes my pain,
You are the breeze that dries my tears.
Jesus I'm so lucky to have You here.

Wendy Forbes

A Prayer To God

Forgive us Father, for we have sinned,
Your gift of life we are destroying.
The goodness in our hearts,
is becoming weaker.
The evil in our minds,
is growing stronger.
Your creation, our home,
is dying because of us.
Please share Your love and grace,
and help us change our ways.
Help remind us of the miracle of life,
by opening our hearts to the beauty of nature.

Amen.

Ann-Marie Wall

MARY, MOTHER OF JESUS

Mary.
A woman.
A woman who looked straight at God, who looked straight back at her.
A woman living in her husband's love.
Mary who said 'Yes' when others hesitated.
In her womb God was encapsulated.
A woman who danced with joy in her soul.
A woman called 'Blessed' by those of the Spirit.
A woman who made mistakes.
A woman who walked, her hand in God's.
A witness of miracles.
A woman whose heart continued to grow, even through pain.
A woman who waited.
A woman - in agony could she understand?
A woman whose heart was pierced.
A woman who was given care of another, to care for her.
A woman who lived to see joy.
A woman on whom God's Spirit was poured out.
A woman to be honoured.
Mary.

Sarah Harris

IN MEMORIAM

In loving memory
The card did read,
Flowers all tied up
With a sombre bow.

The card, the flowers,
Like Mr Stockwell are rotting;
Committed to the earth,
Human becomes humus.

Who would have thought
A little baby boy
Would some day
Grow old and die.

A young vibrant man
Would be the cause of grief,
To those who mourn
His passing from among us.

And why do we bewail?
Is it not that we see how frail
How close we are to death,
Yes - more close with each breath.

I will make my A-Z
A pleasant affair
I will make it a hell
For others and myself.

But all must pass on
Beyond, out of reach,
Save for the cranks
And the love of God.

Gordon Banks

MOST BEAUTIFUL THINGS

The butterflies with their delicate wings
Are numbered in God's most beautiful things
Small bird that sits on the bough and sings
Is one of God's most beautiful things.

Skylark soaring with outstretched wings
Is a pattern of God's most beautiful things.
The bumble bee, and altho' it stings
Is among God's most beautiful things.

flowers that grow by the wayside springs
Are many of God's most beautiful things.
Wild cats in the jungle, with lions and kings
Are truly God's most beautiful things.

A tiny babe and the joy it brings
Is the fullness of God's most beautiful things.
Souls returning to God from their wanderings
Are the greatest of God's most beautiful things.

E M Wollen

NEW LIFE

When Easter is here
Dark days of winter disappear
New life in gardens are picturesque
With golden daffodils and colourful wallflowers
Primroses and violets in woods we find
Celandine, little rays of sunshine
In fields new-born lambs play
With sheep grazing not far away
Rooks building nests in treetops high
The wonder of a baby's first cry
Many blessings, God gives them all
New life, new joy, new beginning
       Praise the Lord.

Audrey Myers

Commended

MAUNDY THURSDAY

I'd turned from Christ that morning
witnessed to my total non-atunement
with the God in him,
faced my own crossing of the ways
and come to fear
poised in an agony.
I prayed for help
knowing I could not further on my own.
I worked
the fear within unsettled
till all at once
I saw
Christ in that week
Palm Sunday left behind
knowing the end to come
prepare
in sweat and tears
the garden
tempted to flee
fear in the throat
mind miasmed
looking for one friend only
who would share
or take away
the cup
the taste
the blood . . .
I wept
and through my tears
inside
I heard my voice say:
'I had no idea'
amazed
and, in reply,

swift, close and comforting
the answer:
'Very few people do'
and I knew Christ in me.

Francesca Greene

Commended

FRAGILE EARTH

The maker of the heavens
First hung the stars above,
To brighten up the backdrop
Of the focus for His love.

This small and wondrous planet,
A golden orb of labour,
Its surface full of beauty
For all that lives to savour.

The secrets of its making
Great scientists unfold.
Answer to the question 'Why?'
God chooses to withhold.

This Earth, so small and fragile,
A gift from God above,
Should be, by us, attended
With great respect and love.

J G Ryder

THE GIFT OF TEARS

Tears, fierce or gentle,
launder heart's pain,
leave its hurt places
refreshed again.
Tears are God-given,
a natural spring
of healing waters,
comforting . . .
Pity then those
who never cry,
or think themselves
too brave to try.

Patricia Butterworth

THE SECRET POOL

Spiritual pool of inner resources,
Which replenishes the tired traveller.
Here lies a veritable oasis,
   Amidst arid desert.
Everyone has their desert days,
And the dark nights of,
   The soul too.
Hopeless feelings of being lost,
   Along life's way.
Spiritual fronds lulled gently,
Cups life giving host,
From pure chalice: lilies,
Renders simple aves.
The gardener is within us.
He gives life to all.

Terri Fisher

THE WREN

Little bird so small and frail
where do you hide when the storm winds blow?
When your home is buffeted to and fro,
Yet when the wind has died away
Your sweet song greets a quieter day
and here again so proud and bright
once more upon the fence alight.
While rain and wind have swept the land
the Lord has held you in His hand.
So how can I in all my fear
fail to feel His presence near,
To wrap me in His cloak of calm
and gently bear me up from harm.

Wendy Skinner

CONQUER THE DARKNESS

I am cold, and I'm alone
the darkness closes in
no one can know the weight of the fears
engulfing every thought and emotion
In my mind I cry, not able nor wanting
to share or express my tears.

I carry on as normal
a smile, the only fragile barrier
between the world and its expectation,
and my psychological warfare,
an unseen battle within a battle
evil rages within God's creation.

I'm awake yet not awake
from sleep that is not sleep
when a warm and calming memory
rises up from deep within
Just a faint glimmer to start with
then the light floods to every part of me.

Be still my child, be still
do not let the darkness conquer you
you have all you'll every need for protection
against the unseen enemy, the twister, the liar
the manipulator who distorts the truth,
him who's engineering this spiritual war's direction.

Put on my armour, hide in me
yet not hide in me but stand up tall!
Strong! Mighty! Able! Glorious!
My promises are true, your *praises* are your power
our spirits joined are a force almighty
able to conquer the darkness, just be victorious!

E A Marshall

IN LITTLE THINGS

The wheat growing high in the cornfield,
The sun shining up above
The birds and the bees, and the flowers,
All tell of our Father's love.

The little mouse in the granary,
The blackbird on the wing,
The sounds of rippling water,
And the beauty in everything.

He is always all around us,
In the little things of life,
If we only stop to listen
Amidst the trouble and the strife.

When life seems to drag us downward,
And we feel tired and worn,
He is there to lift us upward
Towards a bright new dawn.

So as you tread life's journey
Never cease to remember and see
That the God who created all nature
Is the one who made you and me.

June Atkinson

Only One

There is only one figure by the bridge
Where once two lovers met
One heart silent with remorse
One bitter with regret

It is quiet in the afternoon
Where once they softly talked
Only one shadow seen through the trees
Where once two shadows walked

There is only one to feel the cold
Of the October eve
Only one to watch the flames
Left alone to grieve

Andréa Selina Thomas

DEEP WATERS

The river's in spate
Its bed lost in flood.
Acres of meadows
Lush grass spewing mud.

Is this a field gate
Top rail just showing?
Magpies blustering,
Where is the lowing?

Two or three bubbles
Break surface and float,
Last gasps, extinction?
Too late with the boat?

Gaunt arms reach skywards
The trunk is submerged.
Birds fill the branches
As flood waters surge.

Noisily flapping
Protesting a lot,
Evacuating
To high drier spot.

Wet volunteers toil
Save some drowning thing.
There's one ray of hope
A dove's on the wing.

Sidney A Gadd

QUIET DAY AT BURFORD PRIORY

(Come ye apart)
From the everyday cares,
From the need for awareness
Of traffic, children, finances.
The things that distract
That tear at our heart strings
All demanding attention and action.

Come, feel the blessing of silence,
See the snowdrops
Their pure white profusion
Bringing promise of re-birth.
Feel the wind, feel the sun
Accept my blessings
Of water, air and space.

Dear Lord, I accept Your bounty
May I be still and know You.
May Your Precious Blood
Wash away my guilt and impurities.
I accept Your Holy Spirit
Restoring, renewing, remaking.

Cathie Hicks

Untitled

No spoken word,
No sound,
A bluebottle,
At the window
Drones lazily,
And the rise
And fall of your breath
As we kneel together
At the altar rail,
Heads bowed
And hands out held
To receive the bread
And wine together.
I hold my breath
So that we may
Hear the silence.

Rosemary Jacobs

Commended

MY LOST FRIENDS

I feel, as I grow older,
All my best friends, keep slipping away,
And I read of their passing, more often now,
   In the paper, every day.

But still, I have some wonderful memories,
   Of my friends, who have passed on,
And I never shall forget them,
   Even tho', they've gone.

All my friends, were kind, and true,
   And as I sit each day, and ponder,
I know that, we'll all meet again,
   In that *Heavenly Place*, up yonder.

Jean Hendrie

FOREVER IN MY MIND

Realism tells me that you've left me,
The cold voice of authority states,
That you've passed away.
But my mind says you're there.

I still possess the memories that you gave me,
Of the moments we spent together
And they are becoming sweeter with the passing of time.

They can't be corroded or damaged,
Or spoilt by changing circumstances.
They are secure and untainted; locked away.
They won't change, they are eternal.

And I'm thankful,
For those memories are so pleasing.
I no longer dwell on less pleasant thoughts
Or feel hurt or angry because of what is happening to you.

No, you're at peace now and so am I.

You have never felt so real.
Because I find it easy to think of you,
You're no longer retained to one time or place
You're always with me.
Forever in my mind.

Helen Goddard

THE UNKNOWN

A ray of light shone down on me, and a voice from above said I'm
number three.
When your time is up and you're out of luck.
We have to go as we can't pass the buck.
No-one knows if it's good or bad.
As we can't come back, so I guess this is sad.
Our spirits leave us like a spell, and all that is left is an empty shell.
The pain and suffering lets us go,
But I won't know for sure, until it's my turn to go.

Mandy Jayne Moon

All Praise To God

All Praise to God on high we sing
And all our youthful talents bring,
To lay before Thee on this day
Our praise and thanks to Thee we sing.

Help us to serve the ones we love
And offer them our willing heart
In warm response Thy love to meet,
The daily call of Thy command.

Help us to serve the stranger, Lord,
The stranger we meet upon our way.
In warm responsive love to meet
All we see along life's way.

The Lord is King, O earth rejoice
O earth and all ye heavens shall sing
From world to world the joy shall ring
The Lord Omnipotent is King.

Janet Cavill

THE FIRST CHRISTMAS

I wonder how it really was in days of long ago,
The baby in the manger, and was it really so?
The glorious throng of angels the shepherds and the kings
Or is it all a story of charismatic things?

The fulfilment of a prophecy of which the pieces fit
Or where they don't quite correspond are chiselled off a bit,
The suggested recollections of events and ancient lore
And a little myth and magic might tempt the chronicler.

I wonder if the stable was crowded full of folk
Who had journeyed into Bethlehem to pay the Roman's yoke,
And as we look at grottoes and artificial snow
I wonder how it really was in days of long ago.

But then it would not matter if it was well received,
Our God could veil the face of things and it would be believed
And alter our perception of events long ago
Like when He came to Bethlehem to a stable in the snow.

William Edward M Phillips

NE PLUS ULTRA

From beginning of time man has pondered and thought,
And the meaning of life has earnestly sought.
'Why are we here?' he asks, 'What must I do,
To make my life meaningful, useful and true?'

Early philosophers tried to be wise,
Early astrologers looked to the skies,
Science and physics, technology too,
Every century brought something new.

Man sailed round the world, he took flight in the sky.
Faster and faster he found he could fly.
Then surely the ultimate challenge came,
He was hurled into space by a rocket and flame.

But all man has learnt only goes to show,
The lengths to which he is willing to go,
Recklessly doing whatever he can,
Whether or not it is good for man.

Yet sometimes, when touched by something good,
He'll stop and think, and in this mood,
For a moment he'll know the meaning of love,
And that earth was created by God above.

Out of the chaos of earth today,
Good will come and good will stay.

Katy Connell

Commended

MY EVENING PRIMROSE FLOWER!

The heat has been turned up, these last several days!
And, it was a little hard to breathe, cool air anyway!
It was really so oppressive, night time sleep came and left.
The darkness seeming darker, the stillness so heavy, ones brow,
not damp but wet.
The tasks of the day were slow, as one went from room to room.
Fans whirling, pets lethargic, wondering, can we go out soon?
But, early one morning, I glanced through my windows and saw a
glorious sight.
A very large Evening Primrose plant, ablaze - multiplicity of flowers,
large petals proudly lifted to the skies!
I had briefly noticed them,
their flowers exploding early morning and then at night.
I saw they were not influenced, by adverse heat,
or anything extreme, one way, or the other.
Their destiny, to burst into flower, twice a day, a magnificent
yellow colour!
This, they have never failed to do, these past two months or more,
faithfully on time.
And, I can almost check this with my clock and its lovely hourly chime!
And, so this creation, from the Father's loving hand.
A herb so colourful and so wonderfully planned.
Drew my attention, away from the heat extreme.
My eyes not majoring on the degree - but on my Heavenly Father
and my love for Him!

Mary Comley

CHILDREN IN NEED

Their thunder rolled in words of awesome noise.
She shivered, winding a blanket round her frightened form
And drew into her arms some broken toys.
Lightning flashed in screams of wild revile.
She huddled further down to lose the storm,
Trying to shut her ears to the adult strife.
Their hate spilled out reaching their innocent child.
Fear gnawed at her like a hungry worm. Unwilling
Their child who suffered most from their rage fulfilling.
She thought to run away - but where to go?
The world outside is also full of things that harm.
She knew defeat, this child, enveloped in her woe.
But Jesus was there if only she knew,
Suffering with her, if anyone had told her.
Did you?

Mena Faulkner

GIFTS

You are giving me so much, Lord,
in the autumn of my life.
You are opening new doors to me
and letting in the light.
So many things I should have done
and never thought I would.
You gently took me by the hand
and showed me that I could.

I hardly stop to draw a breath
and haven't time to moan.
I know that all you're giving me
is not for me alone.
If I can share a fraction
of the joy that's in my heart,
I'm giving back a little that
you gave me to impart.

These gifts from you are precious, Lord,
and are not given lightly.
Your loving grace has blessed me
and shown me what is and not what might be.
I thank you every day, Lord,
and praise your Holy name.
I know that I will never ever
be the same again.

Joyce Foale

Why?

Why does the world still fight,
and not grow together in Peace.
Why does man hate so much and not believe
in Love.
Why is there so much hurt, so many
children being unloved.
Why is there so much poverty around,
does no one really care.

Why are there bombs and guns, so many
things that can destroy.
Why are so many people being killed, and
so many people left to mourn.
Why does God love us so, yet watched
his own Son die.
Why was he nailed to the Cross, when
we know he did no wrong.

The reason why Jesus died, was that we
could all be,
set free from sin and believe in him.
That is why Jesus was crucified.
So hopefully one day man will say
why did Christ die for me, and we who
believe can say.
Why? Oh why you? Because Jesus loves
you too.

Why then should we be set free, and why
should we believe in you.
The reason why you should believe in him,
is why of course Eternal Life Anew.

M J Cudmore

HE'S COMING BACK

There's a time coming,
Where there will be no more pain,
Be no sorrow,
Be no sickness.

There's a time coming,
When there will be no more death,
No more suffering,
No more distress.

Christ is coming!
We don't know when,
That's not for us to know,
Only God knows the time.

Will you be ready,
When Jesus comes again?
Will you know Him,
As your Saviour and *Lord?*

Call upon His Name,
Be saved,
Don't you want to live forever,
With your Father by your side?

Dawn P Allison

THE RESURRECTION

The tomb of Christ is void today,
Corruption will no more hold sway,
The risen Lord is gone.

The Magdalen wept to behold
The emptiness. Her heart felt cold
And desperately alone.

Then through the mist of tears she saw
A gardener walking on before.
She ran to seek his aid.

'They've taken the Lord's body, so
I beg you tell me if you know
The place where he is laid.'

'Mary,' was all he had to say
To tell her on that glorious day
That he was risen indeed.

Our lives may seem an empty round
Of tasks, where no hope can be found.
Our secret heart may bleed.

But that third day reversed our fate;
Its purpose was to recreate
New life as in the womb.

So may our doubting hearts revive,
Knowing our Saviour is alive,
Out of the empty tomb.

K Maureen Inglis-Taylor

UNTITLED

I close my eyes in silent prayer.
I know that you are waiting there.
I feel the presence of your holiness,
As your spirit falls on me afresh.

O Lord, help me to live in this place,
Until I come before your grace.
Don't let me fall, or be tempted by,
The evil one who is ever nigh.

Throw down the life line to which I'll cling.
Shelter me always beneath your wing.
You are the rock on which I stand.
Don't leave me in the shifting sand.

Let your light show me the way.
Guide my footsteps every day.
Help me Lord, till I see your face.
Filled with glory, in your dwelling place.

A prayer.

Joyce Screeton

FIERY SHEPHERD KING

Like red paint
dropped on wet paper,
spreading out, like blood,
in unforeseen pattern,
Blood shed by Christ,
spreads fiery spirit
patterns in a life.

Sip from the chalice,
taste the wine, remember blood;
This fount that gives power to serve,
in a Yoke that is easy.

With Christ the Yoke is easy;
horse pulling most
takes weight of the plough;
the other yoked horse,
has an easier pull.

Shepherd, your lantern of flame,
lights the path we walk.
Guide us lambs with light.

Shepherd with spiritual fire,
Burn our dross.
Flame bright, lighten our night
with Your pattern of Fire!

Eleanor Ross

JUST THE HEM OF HIS GARMENT

Just a little closer,
An inch or two maybe.
If only I could touch Him,
Then yes, I would be free.

Free of this, the awful plague,
The years of great despair.
Ah! He's just a little closer now,
I'll touch Him if I dare.

I only touched His garment,
The hem alone I felt,
Yet that was just sufficient
To draw Him to myself.

'Who touched?' He asked the crowd.
It shook me through and through.
And yet my lips they answered;
'twas me, in need of You.'

'Your need is great, but answered.'
Was His response to me.
'Your faith has been rewarded,
And yes, you will be free,'

Not only free of pain and shame
For which I'd come to plead.
But now I had a Saviour
To be with me in my need.

I only touched His garment,
The hem alone I felt;
But life is now so different,
I live not for myself.

Dorothy Eadie

INFORMATION

We hope you have enjoyed reading this book - and that you will continue to enjoy it in the coming years.

If you like reading and writing poetry drop us a line, or give us a call, and we'll send you a free information pack.

Write to :-
**Triumph House Information
1-2 Wainman Road
Woodston
Peterborough
PE2 7BU
(01733) 230749**